ALPHABET
BOOK

![DK]

A DORLING KINDERSLEY BOOK

Written by
Lara Tankel Holtz
Art Editor
Melanie Whittington
Production Kate Oliver

First published in Great Britain in 1997
by Dorling Kindersley Limited,
9 Henrietta Street, London WC2E 8PS
Visit us on the World Wide Web at
http://www.dk.com

Copyright © 1997
Dorling Kindersley Limited, London

A CIP catalogue record for this book is
available from the British Library

ISBN 0-7513-5620-4

Colour reproduction by Flying Colours
Printed in Italy by L.E.G.O.

About this book:
When asked to count up letters in this book,
you should only count the ones in the pictures,
and not any that appear in the text or the corners
of the pages. There is also a complete word list at the
back of this book containing every alphabet
object to be found in the pictures.

ALPHABET
BOOK

Photography by Dave King

DORLING KINDERSLEY

London • New York • Stuttgart • Moscow • Sydney

How many aces are under the album? Find four angels.

Can you find two ambulances? Find the aliens from a faraway asteroid.

Look for one artist and four aeroplanes. Can you see the active athletes?

What is Alex's favourite animal? Count five blue As.

Search for a baby brushing his teeth. Spot a bear bib.

Say BOO to the baby under the basket. Look for a banana and a blue boat.

How many babies are building with blocks? Find a baby blowing bubbles.

Can you see a baby with a bare bottom? Find a bee.

Can you find a crown on top of the chunky chocolate?

Find the cereal C on the cloth.

Spot a cheeky cat carrying a cake.

Can you see a colander in the corner? Find a cow.

Can you find five carrots? Count twenty Cs.

Find the dinosaurs who want their dinner. Do you see a doll in a dress?

What does the duck turn to open the door? Spot a disappearing daisy.

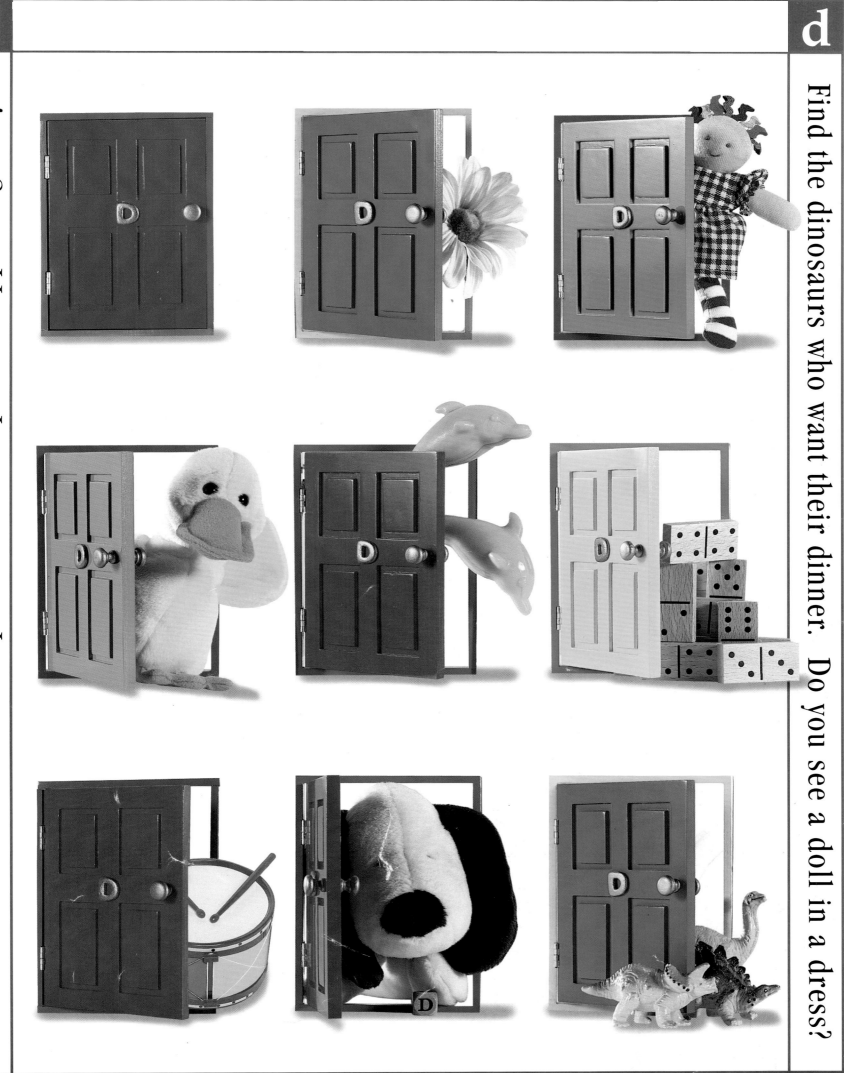

A fly has flown on to the floorboards. Can you find it? Look for a frame.

The flower is made of frayed fabric, fluffy fur, a fern, and what else?

In this green, grassy garden there are lots of animals.

There's a glossy grasshopper, a graceful goose, and a grumpy gorilla.

And there's a giant giraffe gazing over the gate at the gorgeous gazelle.

There's a greedy goat who wants to graze on the grass.

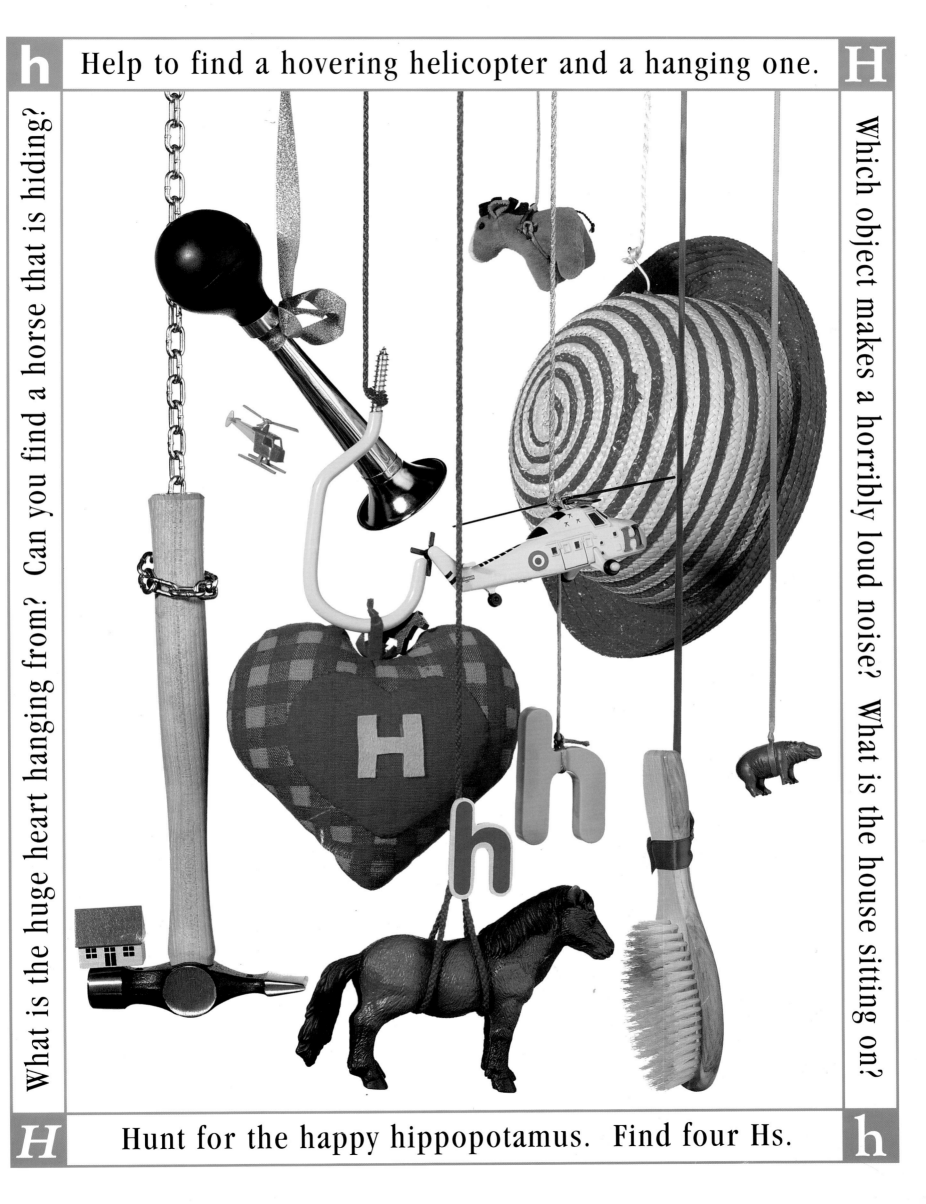

What is the huge heart hanging from? Can you find a horse that is hiding?

Which object makes a horribly loud noise? What is the house sitting on?

Can you help to identify the items imprisoned inside the ice tray?

There's an inviting ice cream and two insects. What else is there?

Try and find a red J, and look for a glass jar.

Now can you find a jaguar? Count twenty jigsaw pieces altogether.

Once upon a time, a kindly king knitted a picture.

He put in two knives from the kitchen and a kangaroo he knew.

And when the picture was finished, the king went out to fly his kite.

He added a big green K and a pink key.

Look for a lobster lying on a ladle, reading a letter.

Locate a lost ladybird. Spot the lively leopard leaping up the ladder.

What is the lamb wearing around her neck? Look for a very large L.

Find an orange lollipop, a lock, and ten ladybirds.

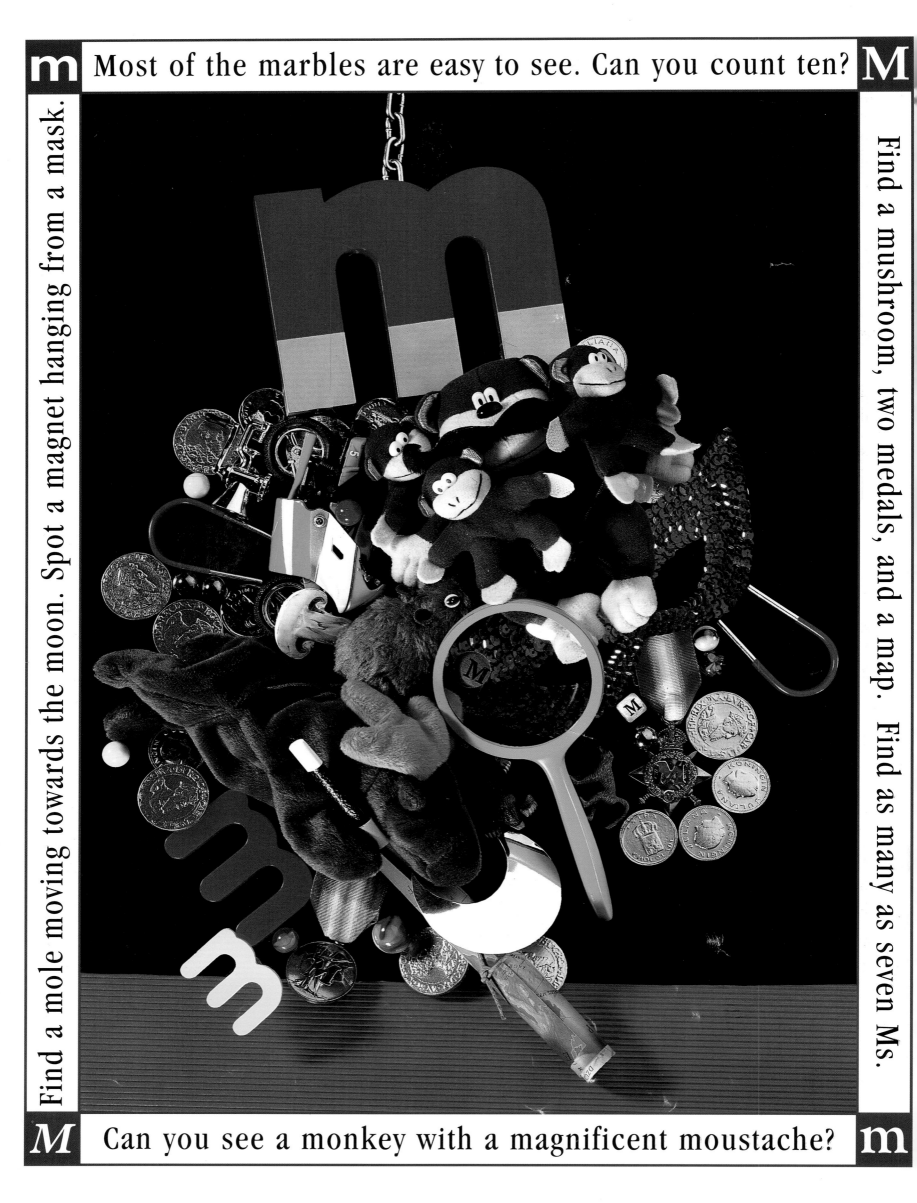

Find a mushroom, two medals, and a map. Find as many as seven Ms.

Find a mole moving towards the moon. Spot a magnet hanging from a mask.

Now, find five number nines. What was used to sew the needlework N?

Where is the nice necklace? Name the wavy N things next to the net.

How many nails can you count? Find ten Ns.

O What is the orang-utan offering the ostrich?

Count four whole oranges. How many legs does the octopus have?

*...*rall, can you find five Os? How many oranges are above the octopus?

O Do you think you can see who the old owl is ogling?

Please look for two party hats. What is on the pirate's shoulder?

Look for the boy in pyjamas. Spot a purse, two pink pigs, and two pandas.

Find a person eating a pizza. Spot two paintbrushes.

The Queen and her quarrelsome quads lay under a quilt.

"I have a quest for you, my quite lovely quadruplets," said the Queen quietly.

A quarter of an hour later the quads were still quarrelling. Can you help?

"How quickly can you find five Qs and a question-mark?"

Can you count sixteen Rs? Find the ravenous rabbit eating a radish.

Where is the rectangle of rice? Can you see four rhinoceroses?

Search for a stamp.

Spot a single seagull and two small sandals.

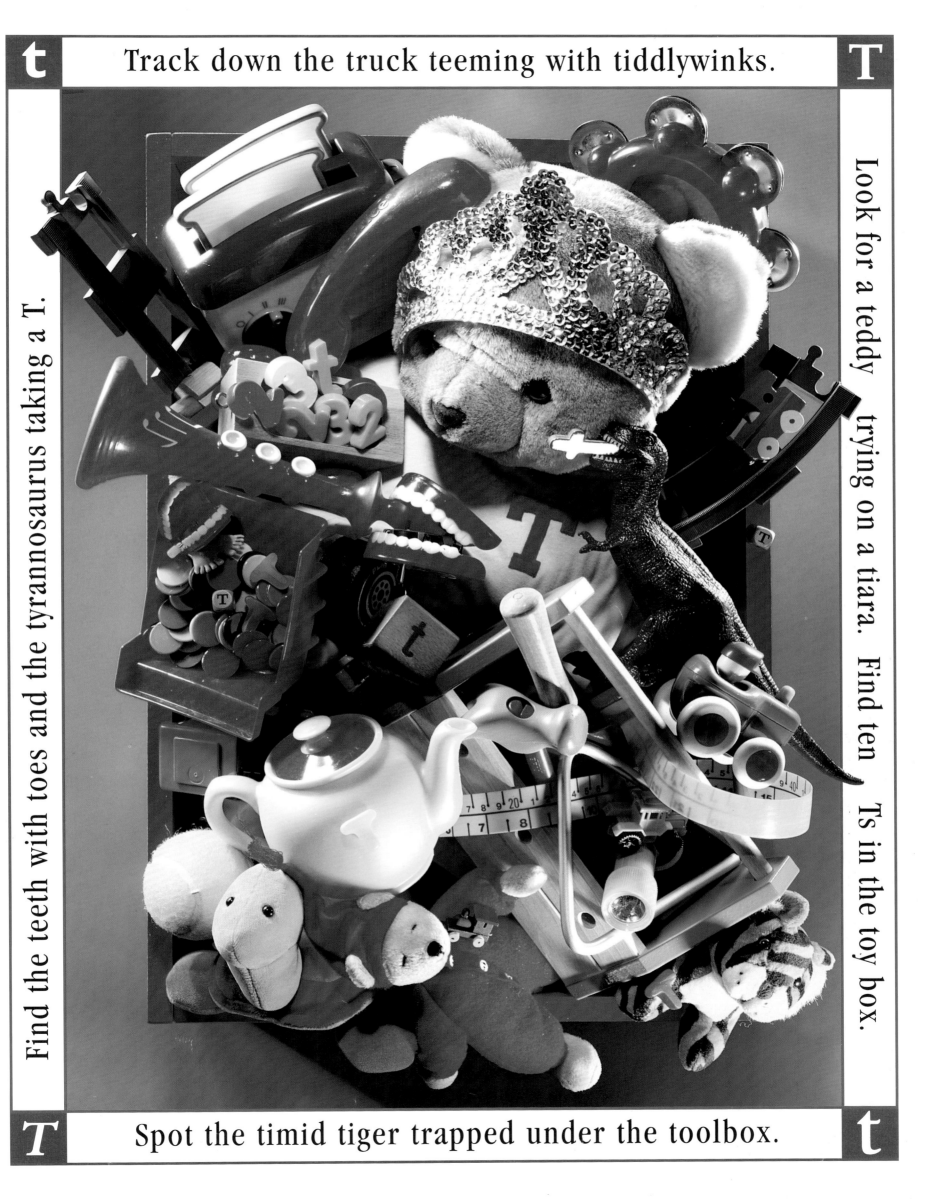

Track down the truck teeming with tiddlywinks.

Look for a teddy trying on a tiara. Find ten Ts in the toy box.

Find the teeth with toes and the tyrannosaurus taking a T.

Spot the timid tiger trapped under the toolbox.

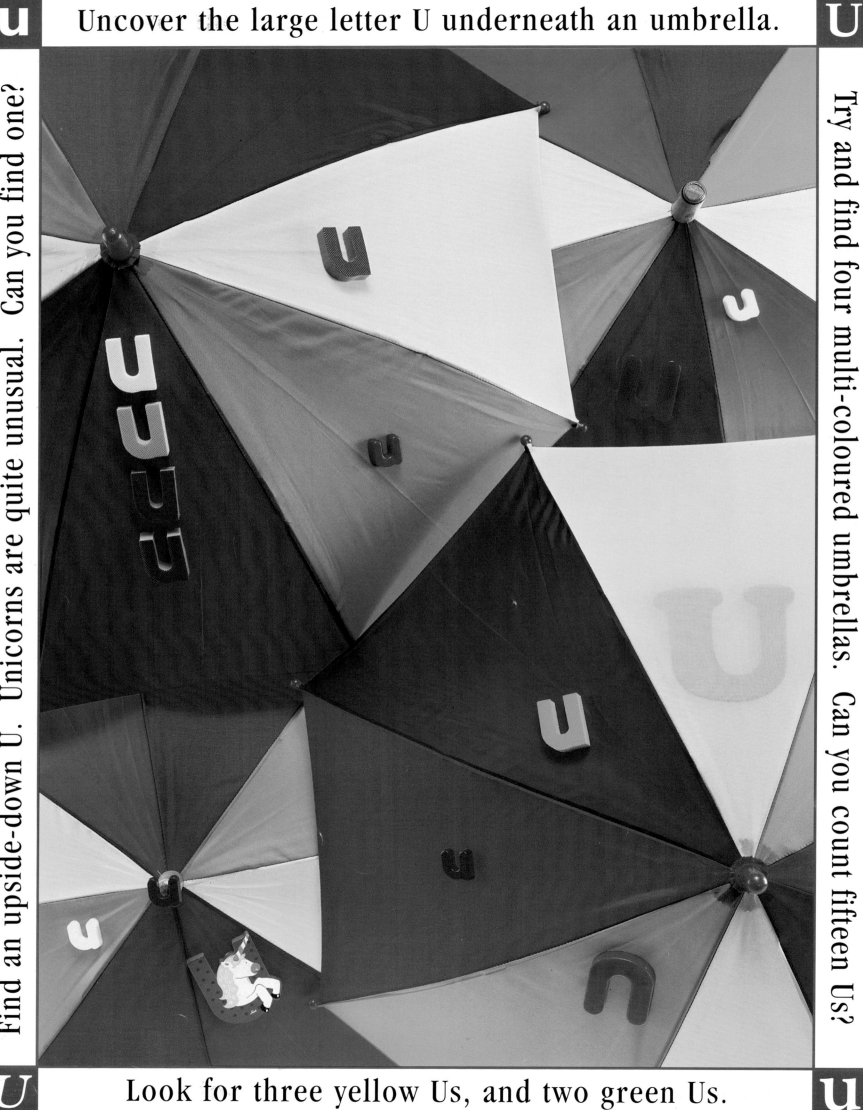

Visit the very vain vampire in his vault ... if you dare.

What musical instrument does he play? Can you find three Vs?

He has a variety of velvet cloaks and his best friend is a bird. What kind?

The vampire loves beautiful violets in a very big vase.

Look for two pieces of watermelon.   What is swimming towards the wire?

Where is the wandering wildebeest?   Can you find a very wet wrench?

X This is an exceptional and extraordinary xylophone. X

With this xylophone, you could play excellent tunes in a music exam.

There are an excessive number of Xs. Can you count twenty-three?

X Have you ever examined an x-ray of a xylophone? X

Try yelling YELLOW YO-YO, RED YO-YO, BLUE YO-YO, GREEN YO-YO.

Now, can you yawn, eat a yummy yoghurt, and also yo-yo at the same time?

A zebra with zest once zoomed away from the zoo.

And he said as he fled, "I'm crazy for Zs, can you help me find six?"

But the zaniest thing by a zillion is a coat you can zip yourself into."

I'm puzzled by zigzags and zombies that snooze.

WORD LIST

Here is a list of the alphabet objects that appear in this book. Can you read the words then find the objects?

A

aces
acorns
aeroplanes
airmail envelope
airship
alarm clock
album
aliens
alligators
ambulances
American flag
anchor
angels
animals
anteater
apples
arks
armadillos
arms
arrow
artist
astronauts
athletes
August
Australia
Australian flag
avocado

B

babies
baby bath
backs
ball
balloon
banana
basket
beads
bee
bib
blanket
blue
boats
books
bootees
bottle
bottom
bubbles
buckets
building blocks
bunny rabbits

C

cakes
candles
card
carrots
cat
cereal
cherries
chocolate
chocolate chips
cinnamon sticks
clocks
cloth
clowns
coconut
coins
colander
cookie cutters
cookies
cornflakes
cow
cream
crowns
crumbs
cube
cup
cup cakes
curls

D

daisy
dinosaurs
dog
doll
dolphins
dominoes
doorknobs
doors
dots
dress
drum
drumsticks
duck

E

Ear Egg
earrings
ears
Earth Egg
eggcups
eggs
Eight Egg
Electric Egg
Elephant Egg
Elevated Egg
Embarrassed Egg
Empty Eggcup
Enormous Egg
Entertainer Egg
Envelope Egg
Evil Egg
Examining Egg
Exercise Egg
Expensive Egg
Exploding Egg
Explorer Egg
Eye Egg
eyelashes
eyes

F

fabric
face
fans
feathers
fern
fish
fives
floorboards
flowers
fly
footprint

fork
fours
frame
frog
fur

G

garden
gate
gazelle
giraffes
goat
gold
goose
gorilla
grass
grasshopper
green glove

H

hairbrush
hammer
hat
heart
helicopters
hippopotamus
hooks
hooves
horn
horses
house

I

ice cream
ice cubes
ice skate
ice tray
insects

iron
island

J

jaguar
jar
jelly
jellybeans
jewellery
jigsaw puzzle
jug
juice

K

kangaroo
key
king
kite
knitting
knitting needles
knives

L

lace
ladder
ladle
ladybirds
lamb
leather
leaves
legs
lemon
leopard
letter
light bulb
lime
lion
lobster

lock
lollipops

M

magic wand
magnets
magnifying glass
map
marbles
mask
medals
metal
mincer
mole
money
monkeys
moon
moose
motorbike
mouse
moustache
mushrooms

N

nails
necklace
needle
needlework
nest
net
nines
noodles
nought
numbers
nuts
(hard-shelled fruit)
nuts
(to screw on to bolts)

O

octopus
orange
oranges
orang-utan
ostrich
owl

P

paintbrushes
paints
pandas
paper
parrot
party hats
patch
pencils
people
pigs
pigtails
pilot
pineapple
pink
pirate
pizza
plaits
plant pots
plants
plate
pockets
popcorn
present
puppets
purple
purse
pyjamas

Q

quadruplets
queen
question mark
quilt

R

rabbits
racing cars
radish
railway tracks
ram
raspberries
rat
recorder
red
reindeer
rhinoceroses
ribbons
rice
rings
robot
rock
rockets
rocking horse
roller skate
rolling pin
rope
roses
rows
rubies
ruler

S

sailing boats
sails
sand
sandals

sandcastles
sea
seagull
sea horses
sea lion
sea urchins
seven
shadows
shark
shells
ships
skull and crossbones
snorkel
S.O.S.
spade
spots
stamp
starfish
submarine
sun
sunglasses
sunhat
sunscreen
surfboard
surfers

T

tambourine
tape measure
teapot
teddies
teeth
telephone
tennis ball
threes
tiara
tiddlywinks
tiger

toast
toaster
toes
toolbox
tools
torch
tortoise
toy box
tracks
tractor
trains
triangle
truck
trumpet
T-shirt
twenty
twos
tyrannosaurus
tyres

U

umbrellas
unicorn

V

vampire
vase
velvet
violets
violin
vulture

W

watch
water
watering can
watermelons
whale

wheels
whisk
whistles
wildebeest
wire
witch
wrench

X

xylophone

Y

yellow
yo-yos

Z

zebra
zip

Dorling Kindersley would like to thank:
The pupils and staff at Summerswood School; James Edwards;

The baby models
Jack D'Cruz, Olivia DeSatge, Sahil Doshi, Charlie Holtz, Ali Miller, Thomas Skinner, Amané Sobue, and Lauren Stanton;

Additional photography
Gary Ombler (letters U, X, Y, Z);

Model makers
David and Sue Donkin, Hot House Models;

Ann Nicol for the clown cake; Rachel Tankel and Sarah Leader for the biscuits and fairy cakes; Jean Horne for the knitting; Milly Eavis for the felt objects; Sarah Charman for the needlework N; Stephanie Spyrakis for the Vampire face; Stephen Goknel for being the Vampire.